The Life and Work of...

Edgar Degas

Jayne Woodhouse

Heinemann Library
Chicago, Illinois

Designed by Celia Floyd
Illustrations by Karin Littlewood
Originated by Ambassador Litho Ltd.
Printed and bound in Hong Kong/China

06 05 04 03 02
10 9 8 7 6 5 4 3 2 1

Library of Congress Cataloging-in-Publication Data
Woodhouse, Jayne, 1952-
  Edgar Degas / Jayne Woodhouse.
     p. cm. -- (The life and work of--)
Includes bibliographical references and index.
Summary: A biography of the nineteenth-century artist, known as one of the French Impressionists.
  ISBN 1-58810-602-0 (lib. bdg.)   ISBN 1-4034-0000-8 (pbk. bdg.)
  1. Degas, Edgar, 1834-1917--Juvenile literature. 2.
Artists--France--Biography--Juvenile literature. [1. Degas, Edgar,
1834-1917. 2. Artists.] I. Title. II. Series.
  N6853.D33 W66 2002
  709'.2--dc21
                        2001003967

Acknowledgments
The author and publishers are grateful to the following for permission to reproduce copyright material:
pp. 4, 18, 22, 24, 28, Bibliothéque Nationale; p. 5, Roger Viollet/Musée d'Orsay, Paris; p. 7, Peter Willi/Musée d'Orsay, Paris; p. 9, Peter Willi/Louvre, Paris; p. 11, Musée d'Orsay, Paris; p. 13, Municipal Museum of Art, Kitakyushu, Japan/Giraudon; p. 15, National Gallery, London; p. 16, Corbis; p. 17, Musée des Beaux-Arts, Pau, France; p. 19, Bridgeman Art Library/Barber Institute of Fine Arts, University of Birmingham; p. 21, Musée d'Orsay, Paris/Giraudon; p. 23, National Gallery of Art, Washington; pp. 25, 27, Christies Images; p. 26, H. Lewandowski/RMN; p. 29, Fitzwilliam Museum, University of Cambridge.

Cover photograph (*Blue Dancers*, Edgar Degas) reproduced with permission of The Art Archive/Musée d'Orsay, Paris/Dagli Orti.

Special thanks to Katie Miller for her comments in the preparation of this book.

Every effort has been made to contact copyright holders of any material reproduced in this book. Any omissions will be rectified in subsequent printings if notice is given to the publisher.

Some words are shown in bold, **like this.** You can find out what they mean by looking in the glossary.

Contents

Who Was Edgar Degas?

Edgar Degas was an important French artist. He used paintings, drawings, **sculpture,** and photography to show his ideas. He became famous for his work.

Edgar lived all his life in **Paris**. His pictures show the people and places he saw around him. His most famous paintings are of ballet dancers. He finished this one when he was 38.

The Dancing Class, about 1873–75

Early Years

Edgar was born on July 19, 1834. He came from a rich family. He was the eldest of five children. When Edgar was a boy, his father, Auguste, often took him to visit art **galleries.**

Edgar's father did all he could to help his son become an artist. Some years later, Edgar painted Auguste as an old man. Auguste loved listening to music.

Lorenzo Pagans and Auguste de Gas, the Artist's Father, about 1871–72

7

Learning to Be an Artist

Edgar studied **law** when he was 19, but he soon gave that up to study art. He loved the work of the painters known as the **Old Masters**. He spent hours copying their paintings to learn from them.

8

Some of Edgar Degas's early pictures were **self-portraits.** Here he is about twenty years old. He shows himself as a well-dressed, shy-looking, young man.

Portrait of the Artist, 1855

Travels in Italy

While in his twenties, Edgar traveled in Italy to learn more about art. He filled many **sketchbooks** with copies of the great paintings he saw there.

The Bellelli Family, 1858–67

In Italy, Edgar stayed with his aunt. He drew
many pictures of his relatives. Later, he used the
pictures to make this painting. Edgar found many
ways to show they were not a happy family.

An Important Meeting

One day in 1862, Edgar was copying a painting in the **Louvre** in **Paris.** There he met an artist named Edouard Manet. They shared many ideas about art and became good friends.

However, Edgar and Edouard sometimes argued. Edgar painted this picture of Edouard and his wife as a gift. He was very angry when Edouard cut out the part he did not like.

Monsieur and Madame Edouard Manet, about 1868–69

Sharing Ideas

Edouard introduced Edgar to other artists whom we now call the **Impressionists.** The artists often met in a café to discuss art. They also held **exhibitions** of their work together.

Edgar's ways of working were very different from the Impressionists, however. He painted detailed images surrounded by large areas of dull color. The focus of his paintings is on people rather than the feel of the whole scene.

Young Girl Being Combed by her Maid, 1876–77

Degas in New Orleans

When Edgar was 38, he visited New Orleans, Louisiana, which is shown here. Members of his family lived there. He stayed at his uncle's house.

The Cotton Exchange in New Orleans, 1873

Edgar painted the cotton office where his relatives worked. His grandfather is seated at the front and his brother is reading a newspaper. This was the first of Edgar's paintings to be bought by an art **gallery.**

Friendships

Edgar never married, but he had close friends he would often visit. These were happy times, as this photograph shows. Edgar is the man on the right.

Some of his friends lived near a **racetrack**. Edgar made many pictures of horses and **jockeys**. This one shows how he liked to paint from unusual viewpoints.

Jockeys Before the Race, about 1878–79

19

Watching Closely

Edgar wanted to show real life as he saw it happening. He always carried a **sketchbook** with him. He used it to write about and draw the things he saw.

Edgar was interested in the lives of everyday people, especially women. In his forties and fifties, he painted workers in a **laundry**. He tried to make the pictures as true to life as possible.

Women Ironing, about 1884–86

Photographs

Photography was invented during Edgar's lifetime. Edgar was always looking for new ideas. When he was about 60, he bought a camera and began to take photographs. He took this one in his **studio**.

Sometimes Edgar traced over his photographs to get the movements of the dancers right. He worked on his pictures for a long time. They often looked like **snapshots** of real life.

Four Dancers, about 1899

Sculptures

Edgar often made models in wax and clay to try out ideas for his paintings. From about 1890, his eyesight began to fail and painting was difficult. **Sculpture** became even more important to him.

This is the only sculpture Degas ever **exhibited.** The dancer is a little taller than a yardstick. She has real hair and wears a real ballet dress and shoes.

The Little Fourteen-Year-Old Dancer, about 1880

Pastels

Edgar liked to work with many different materials. He was one of the few artists of his time to use sticks of color called **pastels**. This box of pastels was found in his **studio**.

This picture of Russian dancers was done in pastels. As Edgar's sight grew worse, the colors he used in his pictures became stronger and brighter.

Russian Dancers, 1899

Edgar's Last Years

For the last five years of his life, Edgar was nearly blind. He stopped working on art. He spent hours each day walking the streets of **Paris.** Edgar was a lonely man. He died in 1917 at the age of 83.

After Edgar's death, people found about 150 wax **sculptures** in his **studio**. Many were later made into **bronze** to display.
Today Edgar's work can be seen in **galleries** around the world.

Ballet Dancer, Bronze

Timeline

1834	Edgar Degas is born in **Paris,** France, on July 19.
1847	Edgar's mother dies.
1853	He studies law for a short time and begins to copy paintings in the **Louvre.**
1855	He studies art at the School of Fine Arts in Paris.
1856–60	Edgar travels in Italy.
1862	He meets Edouard Manet.
1865	Edgar buys a **studio** in Montmartre, in Paris.
1871–72	Edgar travels to London and New Orleans.
1874	His father dies. The first **Impressionist exhibition** takes place.
1877	Edgar becomes friends with the American painter, Mary Cassatt.
1880s	From this time on, he becomes more and more famous. His works are exhibited all over the world.
1890	Edgar moves to a new studio. From now on, his sight becomes worse. He works more in **sculpture** and in pastels.
1895	He begins to experiment with photography.
1912	Edgar moves from his studio. He is now almost blind and stops working.
1914	The start of **World War I.**
1917	Edgar dies on September 27 at the age of 83.

Glossary

bronze   a type of metal

exhibit   to put one's artwork on display for others to see

exhibition   public display of works of art

gallery   room or building where works of art are shown

Impressionists   group of artists who showed the effect of light and movement in their pictures

jockey   person who rides horses in horse races

laundry   place where clothes are washed and ironed

law   rules of a country

Louvre   museum and art gallery in Paris

Old Masters   great artists from Europe who lived a long time ago

Paris   capital city of France

pastels   chalk-like sticks of color used by artists

racetrack   place where people go to see horses racing

sculpture   piece of art made from stone, wood, clay, or metal

self-portrait   picture an artist makes of himself or herself

sketchbook   notepad in which an artist makes rough drawings

snapshot   natural looking photograph taken quickly

studio   room or building where an artist works

World War I   war in Europe that lasted from 1914 to 1918

Index

More Books to Read

Cocca-Leffler, Maryann. *Edgar Degas: Paintings that Dance.* New York: Penguin Putnam, 2001.

Spence, David. *Degas.* Hauppauge, N.Y.: Barron's, 1998.

Venezia, Mike. *Edgar Degas.* Danbury, Conn.: Children's Press, 2000.

More Artwork to See

Ballet Scene. 1907. National Gallery of Art, Washington, D.C.

The Millinery Shop. 1884–90. The Art Institute of Chicago, Illinois.

Race Horses. 1885–88. Metropolitan Museum of Art, New York.